PYGMALION IN MANAGEMENT

Harvard Business Review
CLASSICS

PYGMALION IN MANAGEMENT

J. Sterling Livingston

Harvard Business Press
Boston, Massachusetts

Copyright 2009 Harvard Business School Publishing Corporation
Originally published in *Harvard Business Review* in 1969;
republished in 2002.
Reprint #1768
All rights reserved
Printed in the United States of America

12 11 10 09   5 4 3 2 1

ISBN 13: 978-1-4221-4786-3

The paper used in this publication meets the requirements of the
American National Standard for Permanence of Paper for Publica-
tions and Documents in Libraries and Archives Z39.48-1992.

THE
HARVARD BUSINESS REVIEW
CLASSICS SERIES

Since 1922, *Harvard Business Review* has
been a leading source of breakthrough ideas
in management practice—many of which still
speak to and influence us today. The HBR
Classics series now offers you the opportunity
to make these seminal pieces a part of your
permanent management library. Each volume contains a groundbreaking idea that has
shaped best practices and inspired countless
managers around the world—and will change
how you think about the business world today.

PYGMALION IN MANAGEMENT

In George Bernard Shaw's *Pygmalion,* Eliza Doolittle explains: "You see, really and truly, apart from the things anyone can pick up (the dressing and the proper way of speaking, and so on), the difference between a lady and a flower girl is not how she behaves but how she's treated. I shall always be a flower girl to Professor Higgins because he always treats me as a flower girl and always will; but I know I can be a lady to you because you always treat me as a lady and always will."

Some managers always treat their subordinates in a way that leads to superior performance. But most managers, like Professor Higgins, unintentionally treat their subordinates in a way that leads to lower performance than they are capable of achieving. The way managers treat their subordinates is subtly influenced by what they expect of them. If managers' expectations are high, productivity is likely to be excellent. If their expectations are low, productivity is likely to be poor. It is as though there were a law that caused subordinates' performance to rise or fall to meet managers' expectations.

The powerful influence of one person's expectations on another's behavior has long been recognized by physicians and behavioral scientists and, more recently, by teachers. But heretofore the importance of managerial expectations for individual and group performance has not been widely understood. I have documented this phenomenon in a number of case studies prepared during the past decade for major industrial concerns. These cases and other evidence available from scientific research now reveal:

- What managers expect of subordinates and the way they treat them largely determine their performance and career progress.

- A unique characteristic of superior managers is the ability to create high performance expectations that subordinates fulfill.

- Less effective managers fail to develop similar expectations, and as a consequence, the productivity of their subordinates suffers.

- Subordinates, more often than not, appear to do what they believe they are expected to do.

IMPACT ON PRODUCTIVITY

One of the most comprehensive illustrations of the effect of managerial expectations on productivity is recorded in studies of the organizational experiment undertaken in 1961 by Alfred Oberlander, manager of the Rockaway district office of the Metropolitan Life

Insurance Company. He had observed that outstanding insurance agencies grew faster than average or poor agencies and that new insurance agents performed better in outstanding agencies than in average or poor agencies, regardless of their sales aptitude. He decided, therefore, to group his superior agents in one unit to stimulate their performance and to provide a challenging environment in which to introduce new salespeople.

Accordingly, Oberlander assigned his six best agents to work with his best assistant manager, an equal number of average producers to work with an average assistant manager, and the remaining low producers to work with the least able manager. He then asked the superior group to produce two-thirds of the premium volume achieved by the entire agency during the previous year. He describes the results as follows:

> Shortly after this selection had been made, the people in the agency began referring to this select group as a "super-staff" because of their high esprit de corps in operating so well as a unit. Their production efforts over the first 12 weeks far surpassed our most optimistic expectations . . . proving that groups of people of sound ability can be motivated beyond their apparently normal productive capacities when the problems created by the poor producers are eliminated from the operation.
>
> Thanks to this fine result, our overall agency performance improved by 40%, and it remained at this figure.

In the beginning of 1962 when, through expansion, we appointed another assistant manager and assigned him a staff, we again used this same concept, arranging the agents once more according to their productive capacity.

"The assistant managers were assigned . . . according to their ability, with the most capable assistant manager receiving the best group, thus playing strength to strength. Our agency overall production again improved by about 25% to 30%, and so this staff arrangement remained in place until the end of the year.

Now in this year of 1963, we found upon analysis that there were so many agents . . . with a potential of half a million dollars or more that only one staff remained of those people in the agency who were not considered to have any chance of reaching the half-million-dollar mark.

Although the productivity of the super-staff improved dramatically, it should be pointed out that the productivity of those in the lowest unit, "who were not considered to have any chance of reaching the half-million-dollar mark," actually declined, and that attrition among them increased. The performance of the superior agents rose to meet their managers' expectations, while that of the weaker ones declined as predicted.

Self-Fulfilling Prophecies

The "average" unit, however, proved to be an anomaly. Although the district manager expected only average performance from this group, its productivity increased significantly. This was because the assistant man-

ager in charge of the group refused to believe that she was less capable than the manager of the superstaff or that the agents in
the top group had any greater ability than
the agents in her group. She insisted in dis-
cussions with her agents that every person in
the middle group had greater potential than
those in the superstaff, lacking only their
years of experience in selling insurance. She
stimulated her agents to accept the challenge
of outperforming the superstaff. As a result,
each year the middle group increased its productivity by a higher percentage than the
superstaff did (although it did not attain the
dollar volume of the top group).

It is of special interest that the self-image
of the manager of the average unit did not

permit her to accept others' treatment of her as an average manager, just as Eliza Doolittle's image of herself as a lady did not permit her to accept others' treatment of her as a flower girl. The assistant manager transmitted her own feelings of efficacy to her agents, created mutual expectancy of high performance, and greatly stimulated productivity. Comparable results occurred when a similar experiment was made at another office of the company.

Further confirmation comes from a study of the early managerial experiences of 49 college graduates who were management-level employees of an operating company of AT&T. David E. Berlew and Douglas T. Hall of the Massachusetts Institute of Technology examined the career progress of these managers over a period of five years and discovored that their relative success, as measured by salary increases and the company's estimate of each one's performance and potential, depended largely on the company's expectations.

The influence of one person's expectations on another's behavior is by no means a business discovery. More than half a century ago, Albert Moll concluded from his clinical experience that subjects behaved as they believed they were expected to. The phenomenon he observed, in which "the prophecy causes its own fulfillment," has recently become a subject of considerable scientific interest. For example:

- In a series of scientific experiments, Robert Rosenthal of Harvard University has demonstrated that a "teacher's expectation for a pupil's intellectual competence can come to serve as an educational self-fulfilling prophecy."

- An experiment in a summer Headstart program for 60 preschoolers compared the performance of pupils under (a) teachers who had been led to expect relatively slow learning by their children, and (b) teachers who had been led to believe that their children had excellent intellectual ability and learning capacity. Pupils of the second group of teachers learned much faster.[1]

Moreover, the healing professions have long recognized that a physician's or psychiatrist's expectations can have a formidable influence on a patient's physical or mental health. What takes place in the minds of the patients and the healers, particularly when they have congruent expectations, may determine the outcome. For instance, the havoc of a doctor's pessimistic prognosis has often been observed. Again, it is well known that the efficacy of a new drug or a new treatment can be greatly influenced by the physician's expectations—a result referred to by the medical profession as a placebo effect.

Pattern of Failure

When salespersons are treated by their managers as superpeople, as the superstaff was at the Metropolitan Rockaway district office, they try to live up to that image and do what they know supersalespersons are expected to do. But when the agents with poor productivity records are treated by their managers as *not* having any chance of success, as the low producers at Rockaway were, this negative expectation also becomes a managerial self-fulfilling prophecy.

Unsuccessful salespersons have great difficulty maintaining their self-image and self-esteem. In response to low managerial expectations, they typically attempt to prevent additional damage to their egos by avoiding situations that might lead to greater failure. They either reduce the number of sales calls they make or avoid trying to close sales when that might result in further painful rejection, or both. Low expectations and damaged egos lead them to behave in a manner that increases the probability of failure, thereby fulfilling their managers' expectations. Let me illustrate.

Not long ago I studied the effectiveness of branch bank managers at a West Coast bank with over 500 branches. The managers who had had their lending authority reduced because of high rates of loss became progressively less effective. To prevent further loss of authority, they turned to making only "safe" loans. This action resulted in losses of business to competing banks and a relative decline in both deposits and profits at their branches. Then, to reverse that decline in deposits and earnings, they often "reached" for loans and became almost irrational in their acceptance of questionable credit risks.

Their actions were not so much a matter of poor judgment as an expression of their willingness to take desperate risks in the hope of being able to avoid further damage to their egos and to their careers.

Thus, in response to the low expectations of their supervisors who had reduced their lending authority, they behaved in a manner that led to larger credit losses. They appeared to do what they believed they were expected to do, and their supervisors' expectations became self-fulfilling prophecies.

POWER OF EXPECTATIONS

Managers cannot avoid the depressing cycle of events that flow from low expectations

merely by hiding their feelings from subordinates. If managers believe subordinates will
perform poorly, it is virtually impossible for
them to mask their expectations because the
message usually is communicated unintentionally, without conscious action on their part.

Indeed, managers often communicate
most when they believe they are communicating least. For instance, when they say
nothing—become cold and uncommunica-
tive—it usually is a sign that they are dis-
pleased by a subordinate or believe that he or
she is hopeless. The silent treatment communicates negative feelings even more effectively, at times, than a tongue-lashing does.
What seems to be critical in the communica-
tion of expectations is not what the boss says

so much as the way he or she behaves. Indifferent and noncommittal treatment, more often than not, is the kind of treatment that communicates low expectations and leads to poor performance.

Common Illusions

Managers are more effective in communicating low expectations to their subordinates than in communicating high expectations to them, even though most managers believe exactly the opposite. It usually is astonishingly difficult for them to recognize the clarity with which they transmit negative feelings. To illustrate again:

- The Rockaway district manager vigorously denied that he had communicated low expectations to the agents in the poorest group who, he believed, did not have any chance of becoming high producers. Yet the message was clearly received by those agents. A typical case was that of an agent who resigned from the low unit. When the district manager told the agent that he was sorry she was leaving, the agent replied, "No you're not; you're glad." Although the district manager previously had said nothing to her, he had unintentionally communicated his low expectations to his agents through his indifferent manner. Subsequently, the agents who were assigned to the lowest unit interpreted the assignment as equivalent to a request for their resignation.

- One of the company's agency managers established superior, average, and low units, even though he was convinced that he had no superior or outstanding subordinates. "All my assistant managers and agents are either average or incompetent," he explained to the Rockaway district manager. Although he tried to duplicate the Rockaway results, his low opinions of his agents were communicated—not so subtly—to them. As a result, the experiment failed.

Positive feelings, on the other hand, often are not communicated clearly enough. Another insurance agency manager copied the organizational changes made at the Rockaway district office, grouping the salespeople she rated highly with the best manager, the average salespeople with an average manager, and so on. Improvement, however, did not result from the move. The Rockaway district manager therefore investigated the situation. He discovered that the assistant manager in charge of the high-performance unit was unaware that his manager considered him to be the best. In fact, he and the other agents doubted that the agency manager really believed there was any difference in their abilities. This agency manager was a stolid, phlegmatic, unemotional woman who treated her agents in a rather pedestrian way. Since high expectations had not been communicated to them, they did not understand the reason for the new organization and could not see any point in it. Clearly, the way managers treat subordinates, not the way they organize them, is the key to high expectations and high productivity.

Impossible Dreams

Managers' high expectations must pass the test of reality before they can be translated into performance. To become self-fulfilling prophecies, expectations must be made of sterner stuff than the power of positive thinking or generalized confidence in one's subordinates—helpful as these concepts may be for some other purposes. Subordinates will not be motivated to reach high levels of productivity unless they consider the boss's high expectations realistic and achievable. If they are encouraged to strive for unattainable goals, they eventually give up trying and settle for results that are lower than they are capable of achieving.

The experience of a large electrical manufacturing company demonstrates this; the company discovered that production actually declined if production quotas were set too high, because the workers simply stopped trying to meet them. In other words, the practice of "dangling the carrot just beyond the donkey's reach," endorsed by many managers, is not a good motivational device.

Research by David C. McClelland of Harvard University and John W. Atkinson of the University of Michigan has demonstrated that the relationship of motivation to expectancy varies in the form of a bell-shaped curve.[2]

The degree of motivation and effort rises until the expectancy of success reaches 50%, then begins to fall even though the expectancy of success continues to increase. No motivation or response is aroused when the goal is perceived as being either virtually certain or virtually impossible to attain.

Moreover, as Berlew and Hall have pointed out, if subordinates fail to meet performance expectations that are close to their own level of aspirations, they will lower personal performance goals and standards, performance will tend to drop off, and negative attitudes will develop toward the activity or job.[3] It is

therefore not surprising that failure of subordinates to meet the unrealistically high
expectations of their managers leads to
high rates of attrition, either voluntary or
involuntary.

Secret of Superiority

Something takes place in the minds of
superior managers that does not occur in the
minds of those who are less effective. While
superior managers are consistently able to
create high performance expectations that
their subordinates fulfill, weaker managers
are not successful in obtaining a similar
response. What accounts for the difference?

The answer, in part, seems to be that superior managers have greater confidence

than other managers in their own ability to develop the talents of their subordinates. Contrary to what might be assumed, the high expectations of superior managers are based primarily on what they think about themselves—about their own ability to select, train, and motivate their subordinates. What managers believe about themselves subtly influences what they believe about their subordinates, what they expect of them, and how they treat them. If they have confidence in their ability to develop and stimulate subordinates to high levels of performance, they will expect much of them and will treat them with confidence that their expectations will be met. But if they have doubts about their ability to stimulate subordinates, they will expect less of them and will treat them with less confidence.

Stated in another way, the superior managers' record of success and confidence in their own ability give their high expectations credibility. As a consequence, their subordinates accept these expectations as realistic and try hard to achieve them.

The importance of what a manager believes about his or her training and motivational ability is illustrated by "Sweeney's Miracle," a managerial and educational self-fulfilling prophecy.

James Sweeney taught industrial management and psychiatry at Tulane University, and he also was responsible for the operation of the Biomedical Computer Center there.

Sweeney believed that he could teach even a poorly educated man to be a capable computer operator. George Johnson, a former hospital porter, became janitor at the computer center; he was chosen by Sweeney to prove his conviction. In the mornings, Johnson performed his janitorial duties, and in the afternoons Sweeney taught him about computers.

Johnson was learning a great deal about computers when someone at the university concluded that to be a computer operator one had to have a certain IQ score. Johnson was tested, and his IQ indicated that he would not be able to learn to type, much less operate a computer.

But Sweeney was not convinced. He threatened to quit unless Johnson was permitted to learn to program and operate the computer. Sweeney prevailed, and he is still running the computer center. Johnson is now in charge of the main computer room and is responsible for training new employees to program and operate the computer.[4]

Sweeney's expectations were based on what he believed about his own teaching ability, not on Johnson's learning credentials. What managers believe about their ability to train and motivate subordinates clearly is the foundation on which realistically high managerial expectations are built.

THE CRITICAL EARLY YEARS

Managerial expectations have their most magical influence on young people. As subordinates mature and gain experience, their self-image gradually hardens, and they begin to see themselves as their career records imply. Their own aspirations and the expectations of their superiors become increasingly controlled by the "reality" of their past performance. It becomes more and more difficult for them and for their managers to generate mutually high expectations unless they have outstanding records.

Incidentally, the same pattern occurs in school. Rosenthal's experiments with educational self-fulfilling prophecies consistently demonstrate that teachers' expectations are more effective in influencing intellectual growth in younger children than in older children. In the lower grade levels, particularly in the first and second grades, the effects of teachers' expectations are dramatic. In the upper grade levels, teachers' prophecies seem to have little effect on children's intellectual growth, although they do affect their motivation and attitude toward school. While the declining influence of teachers' expectations cannot be completely explained, it is reasonable to conclude that younger children are more malleable, have fewer fixed notions about their abilities, and have less well established reputations in the schools. As they grow, particularly if they are assigned to "tracks" on the basis of their records, as is now often done in public schools, their beliefs about their intellectual ability and their teachers' expectations of them begin to harden and become more resistant to influence by others.

Key to Future Performance

The early years in a business organization, when young people can be strongly influenced by managerial expectations, are critical in determining future performance and career progress.

In their study at AT&T, Berlew and Hall concluded that the correlation between how much a company expects of an employee in the first year and how much that employee contributes during the next five years was "too compelling to be ignored."[5]

Subsequently, the two men studied the career records of 18 college graduates who

were hired as management trainees in another of AT&T's operating companies.
Again they found that both expectations and
performance in the first year correlated consistently with later performance and success.

Something important is happening in the
first year . . . ,"Berlew and Hall concluded.
"Meeting high company expectations in
the critical first year leads to the internal-
ization of positive job attitudes and high
standards; these attitudes and standards,
in turn, would first lead to and be rein-
forced by strong performance and success
in later years. It should also follow that a
new manager who meets the challenge of
one highly demanding job will be given
subsequently a more demanding job, and
his level of contribution will rise as he re-
sponds to the company's growing expec-

tations of him. The key . . . is the concept of the first year as a *critical period for learning,* a time when the trainee is uniquely ready to develop or change in the direction of the company's expectations.[6]

Most Influential Boss

A young person's first manager is likely to be the most influential in that person's career. If managers are unable or unwilling to develop the skills young employees need to perform effectively, the latter will set lower personal standards than they are capable of achieving, their self-images will be impaired, and they will develop negative attitudes toward jobs, employers, and—in all probability—their own careers in business. Since the

chances of building successful careers with
these first employers will decline rapidly, the
employees will leave, if they have high aspirations, in hope of finding better opportunities.
If, on the other hand, early managers help employees achieve maximum potential, they will
build the foundations for successful careers.

With few exceptions, the most effective
branch managers at the West Coast bank
were mature people in their forties and
fifties. The bank's executives explained that
it took considerable time for a person to gain
the knowledge, experience, and judgment
required to handle properly credit risks,
customer relations, and employee relations.

One branch manager, however, ranked
in the top 10% of the managers in terms of

effectiveness (which included branch profit growth, deposit growth, scores on administrative audits, and subjective rankings by superiors), was only 27 years old. This young person had been made a branch manager at 25, and in two years had improved not only the performance of the branch substantially but also developed a younger assistant manager who, in turn, was made a branch manager at 25.

The assistant had had only average grades in college, but in just four years at the bank had been assigned to work with two branch managers who were remarkably effective teachers. The first boss, who was recognized throughout the bank for unusual skill in developing young people, did not believe that it took years to gain the knowledge and skill needed to become an effective banker. After two years, the young person was made assistant manager at a branch headed by another executive, who also was an effective developer of subordinates. Thus it was that the young person, when promoted to head a branch, confidently followed the model of two previous superiors in operating the branch, quickly established a record of outstanding performance, and trained an assistant to assume responsibility early.

For confirming evidence of the crucial role played by a person's first bosses, let us turn to selling, since performance in this area is more easily measured than in most managerial areas. Consider the following investigations:

- In a study of the careers of 100 insurance salespeople who began work with either highly competent or less-than-competent agency managers, the Life Insurance Agency Management Association found that those with average sales-aptitude test scores were nearly five times as likely to succeed under managers with good performance records as under managers with poor records, and those with superior sales-aptitude scores were found to be twice as likely to succeed under high-performing managers as they were under low-performing managers.[7]

- The Metropolitan Life Insurance Company determined in 1960 that differences in the productivity of new insurance agents who had equal sales aptitudes could be accounted for only by differences in the ability of managers in the offices to which they were assigned. Agents whose productivity was high in relation to their aptitude test scores invariably were employed in offices that had production records among the top third in the company. Conversely, those whose productivity was low in relation to their test scores typically were in the least successful offices. After analyzing all the factors that might have accounted for these variations, the company concluded that differences in the performance of new agents were due primarily to differences in the

"proficiency in sales training and direction" of the local managers.[8]

- A study I conducted of the performance
of automobile salespeople in Ford dealerships in New England revealed that
superior salespersons were concen-
trated in a few outstanding dealerships.
For instance, ten of the top 15 salespeople in New England were in three
(out of approximately 200) of the dealerships in this region, and five of the
top 15 people were in one highly successful dealership. Yet four of these
people previously had worked for other
dealers without achieving outstanding
sales records. There was little doubt
that the training and motivational skills

of managers in the outstanding dealerships were critical.

Astute Selection

While success in business sometimes
appears to depend on the luck of the draw,
more than luck is involved when a young
person is selected by a superior manager.
Successful managers do not pick their subordinates at random or by the toss of a coin.
They are careful to select only those who
they "know" will succeed. As Metropolitan's
Rockaway district manager, Alfred Oberlander, insisted: "Every man or woman who
starts with us is going to be a top-notch life
insurance agent, or he or she would not have
been asked to join the team."

When pressed to explain how they "know" whether a person will be successful, superior managers usually end up by saying something like, "The qualities are intangible, but I know them when I see them." They have difficulty being explicit because their selection process is intuitive and is based on interpersonal intelligence that is difficult to describe. The key seems to be that they are able to identify subordinates with whom they can probably work effectively—people with whom they are compatible and whose body chemistry agrees with their own. They make mistakes, of course. But they give up on a subordinate slowly because that means giving up on themselves—on their judgment and ability in selecting, training, and motivating people. Less effective managers select subordinates more quickly and give up on them more easily, believing that the inadequacy is that of the subordinate, not of themselves.

DEVELOPING YOUNG PEOPLE

Observing that his company's research indicates that "initial corporate expectations for performance (with real responsibility) mold subsequent expectations and behavior," R.W. Walters, Jr., director of college employment at AT&T, contends that "initial bosses of new college hires must be the best in the organization."[9] Unfortunately, however, most companies practice exactly the opposite.

Rarely do new graduates work closely with experienced middle managers or upper-level executives. Normally they are bossed by first-line managers who tend to be the least experienced and least effective in the organization. While there are exceptions, first-line managers generally are either "old pros" who have been judged as lacking competence for higher levels of responsibility, or they are younger people who are making the transition from "doing" to "managing." Often these managers lack the knowledge and skill required to develop the productive capabilities of their subordinates. As a consequence, many college graduates begin their careers in business under the worst possible circumstances. Since they know their abilities are not being developed or used, they quite naturally soon become negative toward their jobs, employers, and business careers.

Although most top executives have not yet diagnosed the problem, industry's greatest challenge by far is to rectify the underdevelopment, underutilization, and ineffective management and use of its most valuable resource—its young managerial and professional talent.

Disillusion and Turnover

The problem posed to corporate management is underscored by the sharply rising rates of attrition among young managerial and professional personnel. Turnover among managers one to five years out of college is almost twice as high now as it was a decade ago, and five times as high as two decades ago. Three out of five companies surveyed by *Fortune* in the fall of 1968 reported that turnover among young managers and professionals is higher than five years ago.[10] While the high level of economic activity and the shortage of skilled personnel have made job-hopping easier, the underlying causes of high attrition, I am convinced, are underdevelopment and underutilization of a workforce that has high career aspirations.

The problem can be seen in its extreme form in the excessive attrition rates of college and university graduates who begin their careers in sales positions. Whereas the average company loses about 50% of its new college and university graduates within three to five years, attrition rates as high as 40% in the *first* year are common among college graduates who accept sales positions in the average company. This attrition stems primarily, in my opinion, from the failure of first-line managers to teach new college recruits what they need to know to be effective sales representatives.

As we have seen, young people who begin their careers working for less-than-competent sales managers are likely to have records of low productivity. When rebuffed their customers and considered by their managers to have little potential for success, the young people naturally have great difficulty in maintaining their self-esteem. Soon they find little personal satisfaction in their jobs and, to avoid further loss of self-respect, leave their employers for jobs that look more promising. Moreover, as reports about the high turnover and disillusionment of those who embarked on sales careers filter back to college campuses, new graduates become increasingly reluctant to take jobs in sales.

Thus ineffective first-line sales management sets off a sequence of events that ends with college and university graduates avoiding careers in selling. To a lesser extent, the same pattern is duplicated in other functions of business, as evidenced by the growing trend of college graduates to pursue careers in "more meaningful" occupations, such as teaching and government service.

A serious "generation gap" between bosses and subordinates is another significant cause of breakdown. Many managers resent the abstract, academic language and narrow rationalization characteristically used by recent graduates. As one manager expressed it to me, "For God's sake, you need a lexicon even to talk with these kids." Nondegreed managers often are particularly resentful, perhaps because they feel threatened by the bright young people with book-learned knowledge that they do not understand.

For whatever reason, the generation gap in many companies is eroding managerial expectations of new college graduates. For instance, I know of a survey of management attitudes in one of the nation's largest companies that revealed that 54% of its first-line and second-line managers believed that new college recruits were "not as good as they were five years ago." Since what managers expect of subordinates influences the way they treat them, it is understandable that new graduates often develop negative attitudes toward their jobs and their employers. Clearly, low managerial expectations and hostile attitudes are not the basis for effective management of new people entering business.

Industry has not developed effective first-line managers fast enough to meet its needs. As a consequence, many companies are underdeveloping their most valuable resource—talented young men and women. They are incurring heavy attrition costs and contributing to the negative attitudes young people often have about careers in business.

For top executives in industry who are concerned with organizational productivity and the careers of young employees, the challenge is clear: to speed the development of managers who will treat subordinates in ways that lead to high performance and career satisfaction. Managers not only shape the expectations and productivity of subordinates but also influence their attitudes toward their jobs and themselves. If managers are unskilled, they leave scars on the careers of young people, cut deeply into their self-esteem, and distort their image of themselves as human beings. But if they are skillful and have high expectations, subordinates' self-confidence will grow, their capabilities will develop, and their productivity will be high. More often than one realizes, the manager is Pygmalion.

NOTES

1. The Rosenthal and Headstart studies are cited in Robert Rosenthal and Lenore Jacobson, *Pygmalion in the Classroom* (Holt, Rinehart, and Winston, 1968), p.11.

2. See John W. Atkinson, "Motivational Determinants of Risk-Taking Behavior," *Psychological Review*, vol. 64, no. 6, 1957, p. 365.

3. David E. Berlew and Douglas T. Hall, "The Socialization of Managers: Effects of Expectations on Performance," *Administrative Science Quarterly*, September 1966, p. 208.

4. Rosenthal and Jacobson, p. 3.

5. Berlew and Hall, p. 221.

6. David E. Berlew and Douglas T. Hall, "Some Determinants of Early Managerial Success," Alfred P. Sloan School of Management Organization Research Program #81-64 (MIT, 1964), p. 13.

7. Robert T. Davis, "Sales Management in the Field," HBR January–February 1958, p. 91.

8. Alfred A. Oberlander, "The Collective Conscience in Recruiting," address to Life Insurance Agency Management Association annual meeting, Chicago, Illinois, 1963, p. 5.

9. "How to Keep the Go-Getters," *Nation's Business*, June 1966, p. 74.

10. Robert C. Albrook, "Why It's Harder to Keep Good Executives," *Fortune*, November 1968, p. 137.

ABOUT THE AUTHOR

J. Sterling Livingston was on the faculty of Harvard Business School from 1941 to 1971. He founded the Sterling Institute, a management consulting firm specializing in executive training and development, in 1967 and served as chairman of the Washington, DC–based institute until 1998. He has also established the Sterling Center for Applied Managerial Leadership in Key Biscayne, Florida.

ALSO BY THIS AUTHOR

Harvard Business Review Article

"The Myth of the Well-Educated Manager"

Article Summary

The Idea in Brief

Consider this bold experiment: A branch manager at Metropolitan Life Insurance Company assigned top agents to his best assistant manager, average producers to an average manager, and low performers to the poorest manager.

Surprisingly, the average group enhanced its productivity by a *higher* percentage than the top group. How? Its manager didn't see herself or her agents as average. She told her people they had *more* potential than the "superstaffers"—then challenged them to outperform them.

Her story affirms a vital lesson: When managers *expect* the best from employees, they *get* the best. And when they expect the worst . . . well, they get that, too. The expectations/behavior connection has stimulated research since 1969, when this article was first published. But evoking positive self-fulfilling prophecies is still remarkably difficult. The following guidelines can help.

Idea in Practice

To unleash the power of positive expectations:

- *Don't overcommunicate* negative *feelings.* Managers often communicate low expectations far more effectively than high expectations, for example, through "silent treatments."

- *Clearly communicate* positive *feelings.* If subordinates can't perceive your high expectations, they can't *fulfill* them.

Example: When one manager tried to replicate the Metropolitan experiment, she didn't tell the supervisor of the high-performance unit that she considered him the best. The group's performance never improved.

- *Set realistic expectations.* Subordinates won't work to achieve their best unless they view your expectations as achievable. In one manufacturing firm, production actually *declined* when quotas were set too high.

- *Expect the most from* yourself. Superior managers have confidence in their own ability to select, train, and motivate subordinates. Their confidence influences their beliefs about their employees—and their expectations and treatment of them.

  Managers' self-confidence gives their high expectations *credibility*. Subordinates who view their managers as credible consider their expectations *realistic*—and strive to fulfill them.

Example: James Sweeney, Tulane University
professor and computer-center director,
believed he could teach even poorly educated individuals to operate computers. He
selected custodian George Johnson to prove
his conviction. Thanks to Sweeney's beliefs
about his own teaching powers and Johnson's learning ability, Johnson mastered
the material, began managing the main computer room, and ultimately trained new
employees.

- *Seize advantage of employees' critical first
year.* Your expectations exert their greatest
impact during employees' first year on the
job. As subordinates mature, their aspirations—and your expectations—become col-
ored by past performance. After year one, it's
hard to generate high expectations unless
employees have outstanding records.

- *Make your best managers new hires' first bosses.* A young person's first boss is likely to exert the strongest influence on his or her career. Put your best managers in charge of new college hires.

Example: The most effective branch managers at a West Coast bank were in their forties and fifties—except for one 27-year-old. His first boss had made him a branch manager at 25 because he didn't believe it took years to become an effective banker. His talented protégé quickly excelled *and* trained his own assistant to assume responsibility early.